Arthur Ransome's East Anglia

SWALLOWS·AND·AMAZONS·FOR·EVER!

To the Revd Victor Steynor, in memory of the days we spent exploring

Arthur Ransome's East Anglia

A search for Coots, Swallows and Amazons

by Roger Wardale

with extracts from the original stories by Arthur Ransome

Poppyland Publishing

Frontispiece

A White Boat rounds the mark by Horning Swan, c.1927

The 'Flash' had rounded a mark too close and touched it and so was out of her race.

Coot Club

(Photo: courtesy George Southgate)

By the same author:

Arthur Ransome's Lakeland
Published by The Dalesman Publishing Company Ltd,
Clapham,
Lancaster, LA2 8EB

Cover photograph: Horning Staithe

Unless otherwise stated, all photographs are from the collection of or by the author.

© Roger Wardale 1988
Published by Poppyland Publishing, North Walsham, Norfolk NR28 9JX
Printed by Printing Services (Norwich) Ltd
Typesetting by PTPS, Norwich
First published 1988
ISBN 0 946148 34 1

Contents

Acknowledgements..6

Introduction...7

Arthur Ransome...9

The Background to the Stories..13

In the Wake of *Titmouse*, *Teasel* and the *Death and Glory*.....21

In the Wake of *Goblin, Wizard* and the *Death and Glory*.........25

The Northern Broads..31

Pin Mill..51

The Walton Backwaters..59

Bibliography...64

Acknowledgements

Without the help and enthusiasm of a number of people, this book would not have been completed, and I am very grateful to the following, all of whom may rightly claim to have a part in it.

It was Anthony Colwell of Jonathan Cape who suggested that I should write about the East Anglian settings. The Rev Victor Steynor put me in touch with possible publishers. Later he laid the foundation for the Harwich and Felixstowe exploration and took photographs.

Sir Rupert Hart-Davis and John Bell allowed me to include extracts from the four books which accompany most of the photographs.

Brigit Sanders expanded a letter she had written to me about her visit to Secret Water so that it might be included, and she photographed a painting her mother had made of her as a child. Gillian Beevor told me about the days she and her family spent with the Ransomes before the war and lent me a photograph of herself with Arthur Ransome looking across the lake to Kanchenjunga. I was much encouraged by the interest of these two 'originals'.

Hugh Brogan has kindly agreed to the *Coot Club* extract from *The Life of Arthur Ransome* being included here, and Christina Hardyment made things easier by sending me some of the correspondence from readers of *Arthur Ransome and Captain Flint's Trunk*.

George Southgate has been my link with Horning and the Broads and his local knowledge and photographs have been invaluable. In Harwich, Richard Woodman was my mentor. In Secret Water, Martin Lewis explored so thoroughly he seems to have covered every yard of it and he sent me a copy of the illustrated log of his voyages of exploration. He also lent me a precious photograph of the *Pommern* which Arthur Ransome had given him.

Up in Leeds Ann Farr and Christopher Sheppard looked through many photographs by Arthur Ransome in the Brotherton Collection in search of the sort I needed, and which the University Library have allowed me to use.

John Berry, who knew both Arthur Ransome and Ernest Altounyan towards the end of their lives, shared his memories with me. In particular, he recalled his adventures when sailing with his family on the Broads in 1939 in the yacht *Mavis*.

My contact in Pin Mill has been Ron Watts who lives in part of Alma Cottage. Others who have helped me include, Sam King, Jim Searle of the Norfolk County Sailing Base; Michael Rines, the Norfolk Naturalists Trust, the Great Yarmouth Port and Haven Commissioners and the Broads Authority. Finally, Margaret Minty made sense of my wild typing and alterations when she produced the final typescript.

Introduction

The haunting sound of Shenandoah played on the radio at tea-time on several occasions during the war meant that "Uncle Mac" was about to read another instalment of *The Big Six* to BBC Children's Hour listeners. That was my introduction to the books of Arthur Ransome and *The Big Six* has remained my favourite.

The wartime paper shortage meant that copies were almost unobtainable and my mother paid regular visits to the Public Library to renew my current Ransome and occasionally, when one was available, to exchange it. Eventually all twelve volumes stood in my bookcase and were frequently read. As soon as it was possible to do so, we went for a holiday to the Lake District to see if the country of the books really existed. We saw enough that week to suggest it did, so when we returned home I wrote to Arthur Ransome to ask him if the places were real and if they were, please would he tell me where I could find them. It was the sort of letter he must have received by the dozen from young admirers, but he courteously answered it.

"The only way to keep a secret (your own and other people's) is NEVER to answer a question. But you seem good at guessing. All the places in the book are to be found but not arranged quite as in the ordnance maps. You seem to be just the reader for those books. I am glad you like them. With best wishes from Arthur Ransome."

I felt that there was a challenge in the reply and I was determined to be equal to it. For more than 30 years I spent most of my holidays in the Lake District and part of each holiday was devoted to "Ransome hunting" I recorded each success with photographs and eventually, with some help from others, I found all the sites and it occurred to me that it might be worth publishing. Encouraged by Christina Hardyment who had just had *Arthur Ransome and Captain Flint's Trunk* published, and Anthony Colwell of Jonathan Cape, Ransome's publisher, I went ahead, found a publisher and in 1985 I met the four people who were the basis for the main characters in the stories and went aboard *Amazon*. My Lakeland quest was complete.

A couple of years after my first visit to the Lakes we spent a week at Wroxham in Norfolk. I was delighted to find that Arthur had not jumbled the Broadland topography, and I could enter the world of the Coot Club in reality and not, as in the Lake District, only be exercising the imagination. Horning Staithe was just as he had pictured it and overlooking the river was the dentist's window in Banham's boatshed. My collection of photographs now included the northern Broads. I have spent a further half-dozen holidays in Norfolk and have seen it change more than the Lake District. I wonder if anyone visiting the area now for the first time feels they are in the world of the Coots? I hope so. Much that Arthur loved - the wild rivers and hiding places in the dykes, the herons and bitterns and fish - can be found, but it is best to visit the area out of the holiday season.

Apart from the 13 stories, four books have been important. Taqui Altounyan's *In Aleppo Once* tells of her childhood in Syria and how they found themselves in an early copy of *Swallows and Amazons* sent by their "Uncle Arthur". Arthur's autobiography reveals much of his early life and influences, but ends as it becomes clear, in the 1930s, that the Swallows books are going to be a success. Hugh Brogan's *The Life of Arthur Ransome* explains how the stories are thinly disguised non-fiction and Christina Hardyment visited many of the places for *Arthur Ransome and Captain Flint's Trunk* and included extracts of unpublished writing.

During the spring of 1988 I managed to revisit almost all the sites mentioned. I was shown around Riverside Cottage (once part of Alma Cottage) at Pin Mill, visited King's Boatyard, sailed on the Harwich-Felixstowe Ferry, and had tea with a most civilised savage while she told me how her family had explored Secret Water more than 50 years before.

The majority of the photographs which I have taken over a period of 30 years aim to show the places as they appeared at that time; or an nearly as possible. Other photographs provide a record of places which have changed. The photographs taken by Arthur and Evgenia Ransome are particularly valuable. Not only do they show how things were in their time, but they also allow us to eavesdrop, as it were, on their cruises.

(right) **Daisy and Captain Flint look across the lake to Kanchenjunga. Arthur Ransome and Gillian Beevor at Coniston about 1947.**

(Photo: Gillian Beevor)

Arthur Ransome

The Ransomes were an East Anglian family. Arthur traced his Quaker ancestors back as far as a Norwich miller in the sixteenth century. Arthur's great-great-grandfather left the area and became a well-known Manchester surgeon but his brother remained to start the Ipswich firm of Ransome and Rapier.

Arthur was born in Leeds in 1884 where his father was Professor of History at the Yorkshire College, now the University of Leeds. Cyril Ransome spent the term lecturing and writing but he was a countryman at heart with a passion for the Lake District and country pursuits. Until his death, which occurred when Arthur was only 13, the family spent the long summer vacation on an isolated farm near the foot of Coniston Water in the Lake District. While the professor fished for pike or sea trout his young family were free to explore what Arthur described as Paradise. They made friends with the Lake Country folk and joined in the rural activities. The children played in or on the lake and some days they picnicked on the island nearby. That island has become a place of pilgrimage for Ransome admirers, some of whom have crossed the world to realise a childhood ambition and land in Wild Cat Island's secret harbour.

His father's death brought a temporary halt to Ransome's Lake District holidays and left him with a guilty feeling of relief, for the two did not hit it off. His father despaired with what he saw as his son's irresponsibility and muffishness.

Arthur, who loved and admired his father, had looked in vain for his approval. He was a sensitive and rather wilful small boy, in some ways like the Roger of his stories. He spent several bitterly unhappy years at prep school in Windermere before going to Rugby. It was not until he was at Rugby that the teachers found he was very short-sighted. This unsuspected disability was soon corrected by spectacles and Arthur started to enjoy life at school. He had been writing stories since he was eight and he began to consider it as a career. However, perhaps to satisfy his mother who wanted her eldest son to find a safe job, he left to read science at the Yorkshire College.

His university career lasted just two terms and he was still only 17 when he went off to London to become errand-boy to the publishing company of Grant Richards. But Arthur had no intention of becoming a publisher and after six months he had joined the failing Unicorn Press which gave him the opportunity to write stories and articles for newspapers. Next he found a job as a ghost-writer of sporting books and the first book to appear under his own name was *The ABC of Physical Culture* published in 1904. This was followed by such titles as *The Soul of the Streets*, *The Stone Lady* and *Highways and Byways* in Fairyland. In 1907 the largely autobiographical *Bohemia in London* was published and was his first success.

He enjoyed his Bohemian life in the capital with regular holidays in the Lake District where he was befriended by W

G Collingwood, the Coniston artist, writer and historian, and his family. They gave Arthur just the sort of encouragement as a writer that he needed and had failed to find in his own family. The younger Collingwoods, Barbara, Dora and Robin were near enough his own age to be good companions and he came close to marrying Barbara. Years later Dora's children were to be the models for his Swallows and Amazons.

In 1909 he fell under the spell of Ivy Walker and they married. Arthur almost immediately regretted it, for Ivy was a woman of wild fantasies who made his life unbearable. He loved their only daughter, Tabitha, but in 1913 after Ivy had refused to consider a divorce, he realised he must get away. He had always been interested in fairy stories and he had enjoyed the Jamaican folk tales he heard in London. He decided that Ivy would not be able to follow him to Russia where he could collect fairy stories to translate for English children to enjoy. The result was *Old Peter's Russian Tales* which has been hugely successful and has remained in print ever since it was published in 1916. There are those among his readers, including one of his original Swallows, who prefer it to his Swallows stories. In 1984 a second volume was published under the title of *The War of the Birds and the Beasts and other Russian Tales*.

He remained in Russia during the Great War as correspondent for the Daily News and then covered the Russian Revolution as special correspondent for the Manchester Guardian. He became close to the Bolshevik leaders and played chess with Lenin in the Kremlin. He felt it was his mission to keep the peace between the Soviets and England and acted as a go-between between the Foreign Office and the Bolsheviks who recognised his unique position and took advantage of it. His duties brought him into regular contact with Trotsky's secretary who issued bulletins from his office. She was Evgenia Petrovna Shelepina and soon they fell in love. Evgenia was a large, loyal, warm-hearted and warm-tempered lady who was to become Arthur's constant companion and severest critic.

In 1920 they stayed in Reval in Estonia enjoying a little sailing. Ivy still refused to divorce him and so they remained in eastern Europe. In 1922 he had the ketch *Racundra* built in Riga in the Baltic and the story of their first voyage has become a classic of its kind.

At last in 1924 Ivy agreed to a divorce and he was free to return to England and marry Evgenia. They hurried back and settled in a remote and primitive cottage near Windermere. In order to buy it they had, with much regret, to sell *Racundra* to Adlard Coles, the yachting writer. The cottage offered good opportunities for sailing and fishing and the Manchester Guardian kept Arthur busy, sometimes sending him on trips abroad. He was never fully reconciled to journalism and the turning point in his life came in 1928. Dora Collingwood had married Ernest Altounyan, another of Arthur's friends and they returned from Syria for the summer with their young family. The children learned to sail on Coniston Water and it was an unforgettable summer. This gave Arthur the inspiration to write *Swallows and Amazons*. Arthur was never happier than while writing it, but before it was completed he found he could not combine journalism and fiction writing. Loyally supported by Evgenia he resigned from the paper and agreed in future to contribute only on a freelance basis. The publication of *Swallows and Amazons* in 1930 was a landmark in children's fiction and it was quickly followed by four sequels.

At this time Arthur weighed around 17 stones. He looked very fit but he was troubled by a duodenal ulcer and other internal problems. It was partly because cruising always had a beneficial effect upon Arthur's health that in 1935 the Ransomes began to look for a house on the east coast. After some searching they rented Broke Farm, Levington, across the River Orwell from Pin Mill. They quickly bought a seven-ton cutter they renamed *Nancy Blackett*. They had never forgotten the days they had with *Racundra* and hoped to recapture them in their new boat. They became part of the sailing community based at Pin Mill and cruising in *Nancy* brought Arthur two books, but Evgenia thought the galley was too small and in 1938 Harry King, the Pin Mill boatbuilder, built him a larger boat. *Selina King* was designed by Fred Shepherd as a roomy cutter 35ft o.a. She was a splendid yacht, but world war two prevented them from having more than a few months sailing. Just before the outbreak of war they moved across the river to Harkness Hall.

Soon the Battle of Britain was taking place overhead and the disturbed nights bothered Evgenia. They decided to return to the Lakes and bought a bungalow beside Coniston Water. *Selina King* was laid up for the duration of the war. Arthur enjoyed the return to the Lakes and produced his final Lakes book, but Evgenia hated it and as soon as the war was over the bungalow was sold and they were back house-hunting in Suffolk. This time they were not successful and for the remainder of their lives they moved house between London and the Lakes and back again. When he was able to sail again it was thought *Selina King* was too large for Arthur to handle and he parted with her. Laurent Giles designed a smaller boat to replace her.

Peter Duck is an eight ton ketch and was built by Harry King in 1946. The design proved very popular and more than fourteen yachts of the *Peter Duck* class have been built.

Finally, when he was 69, Arthur went to David Hillyard, who had built *Nancy Blackett* and bought one of his five-ton sloops. *Lottie Blossom* was kept in Chichester Harbour and he sailed her long after his doctor had told him to stop.

The Swallows series was completed in 1947. The books had an enormous success in this country and have been translated into 13 foreign languages, including Chinese.

In 1937 *Pigeon Post* had received the first Carnegie Medal for the best children's book of the year and in 1951 he was made an honorary D Litt by the University of Leeds. He was greatly pleased by this and from that time he was always Dr Ransome. Finally in 1953 he received the C B E. The Ransome's last home was yet another remote cottage in the Lakes, not far from the scene of his childhood holidays. Arthur died in 1967 and Evgenia seven years later.

Arthur Ransome, by the author.

Witch's Quay, 1975

Long years ago there must have been busy barge traffic in and out from this old quay when there were no railways and poor roads and everything that could be was carried by water.

Secret Water

The Background to the Stories

The story of *Swallows and Amazons* began with Arthur's holidays at Coniston as a child and grew out of the happy summer of 1928 when he and Ernest Altounyan bought two 13-foot dinghies for the young Altounyans to learn to sail. When they had returned to Syria and he was sailing the *Swallow* on Windermere, Arthur set to work on a story which was to remind them of their holiday. He remembered his own childhood holidays and put the Altounyans into the story with their boats and their "Uncle Arthur" thinly disguised as Captain Flint.

The Swallows or Walker children were mostly Altounyans. The exception was John, the eldest. John was the steady and capable boy who would have pleased his own father and who, looking back, Arthur would like to have been. Susan was Susie, and probably a little too good. Susie was interned by the Germans when she was caught in France during the war. She now lives there, married to a Frenchman. Titty, whose real name, Mavis, is never used in the stories or by family and friends, is the artistic and imaginative member of the family. She lives just across the lake from where they learnt to sail sixty years ago. The late Roger Altounyan was a keen sailor and fisherman. After distinguished service as a pilot in the war, he qualified and joined his father and grandfather in Syria where they ran a hospital in Aleppo. His later career was spent on research. An asthma sufferer himself, he developed the Intal treatment and the spin-haler which have given relief to millions of other sufferers throughout the world. Bridget is

Brigit Sanders (nee Altounyan) who lives in a cottage next to the farm where Arthur stayed almost a hundred years ago. A short distance away by the lakeshore a dinghy waits for the explorers among family and friends. Commander Walker owed something to Ernest Altounyan who may even have sent the famous telegram at the start of the story. Certainly it was very much his way of doing things.

The Amazons, Nancy and Peggy Blackett, have no such easily recognised originals. All Arthur himself said was that he remembered two girls playing by the lake wearing red caps. I believe the answer lies with Taqui - the eldest of the Altounyan girls. Because there were too many girls in the family Taqui was thought to have been turned into John. But the lively, adventurous Taqui was much too interesting a child to have been left out of the story, so Arthur used her as a model for Nancy Blackett, the terror of the seas. He was always susceptible to tomboys and in Nancy he created the ideal tomboy who became very real to him. Peggy, the most lightly drawn of the main characters, has no original.

Its sequel, *Swallowdale*, followed in 1931, but already he was planning something altogether different. In *Peter Duck* his Swallows and Amazons are involved in a fantasy about desert islands, buried treasure and pirates. The story of the voyage to a Caribbean island was supposed to have been made up by the Swallows and Amazons and Captain Flint on board a wherry on the Broads during the winter holidays. It is not clear when

Arthur made his first visit to the Broads. In 1919 he spent part of the summer in England and went fishing in Norfolk. Ernest Altounyan, who had met Arthur around 1903, claimed to have taught him to sail tacking along the rivers of the Broads. Ernest was a great Broads enthusiast and he almost certainly introduced Arthur to the area before he took his family out to Aleppo in 1919.

In her book *Arthur Ransome and Captain Flint's Trunk* Christina Hardyment includes an extract of an early draft of *Peter Duck* entitled *Their Own Story* which gives a very different treatment. The story switches between the winter world of Broadland and the fantasy voyage and it is clear that Arthur was right in abandoning it in favour of the version which some adults (but not the present writer) consider his finest achievement.

The treasure-hunting voyage begins and ends at Lowestoft and Arthur made a point of visiting the port to make sure of the accuracy of his portrait. He also visited Pin Mill where he had the dinghy called *Peter Duck* built for him to take out to Syria when they visited the Altounyans in 1932. Much of *Peter Duck* was written during that visit. Arthur wrote to his mother that it felt a little queer after living with them in *Swallows and Amazons* and *Swallowdale* to meet once more as actual human beings running about.

The old seaman after whom the book is named appeared in *Racundra's First Cruise* as the Ancient Mariner. He met the Ransomes when he looked after their dinghy in a tiny port near Riga in Latvia, where he was harbourmaster. He had indeed sailed in the *Thermopaly* and just as Peter Duck asks to join the crew of the *Wild Cat* he had asked to sail in *Racundra* so he could go to sea once more before it was too late. Arthur enjoyed introducing Bill, the red-haired boy who claimed to have been born on the Dogger Bank. He thought him rather a lark and a welcome change from the others. Most of all he enjoyed developing the characters of Captain Flint and Peter

Duck and the contrast between the simple dignity of the former Cape Horn seaman and the impetuous, romantic Captain Flint is one of the joys of the book.

In *Winter Holiday* he was back in the Lake District with a story which looked back to his schooldays by Windermere when the lake froze over during the great frost of 1895. He looked back in another way, for when he introduced two delightful characters he gave them some of his youthful characteristics. Dorothea is a literary romantic and her younger brother Dick is a practical and resourceful scientist given to consuming enthusiasms. Arthur found them very entertaining companions and when talking with friends would introduce them into the conversation as if they existed.

In 1931 the Ransomes hired the yacht *Winsome* from Herbert Woods of Potter Heigham and in 1933 they were back again, this time in a Fairway. About this time Arthur was resolved to write a story set on the Broads. He was always responsive to landscape and he was charmed by the slow-moving rivers and little dykes full of all sorts of hiding places. He had a notion of a plot with two priggish town children and a group of local children. Its title, *Webfooted Grandmother*, referred to a lively old lady, in marked contrast to Nancy and Peggy's Great Aunt. It was some time before he took up Genia's suggestion to replace the priggish ones with Dick and Dorothea. It is clear from *Coot Club* that with Arthur the setting came first, the characters second, followed by incidents and finally the plot.

Once he had decided that the story could unfold through the eyes of Dick and Dorothea his imagination raced ahead and in April 1934 they went for a cruise to all the places in the story and took a set of photographs from which illustrations could be drawn. The result was that *Coot Club* is the best illustrated book in the series, full of charming tailpieces and accurate draughtsmanship.

The D's meet Tom Dudgeon, the Horning doctor's son, on the train to Wroxham. They discover that birdwatching and sailing occupy all his spare time. They meet again later that day when Tom hides in the reeds beside the yacht the D's are using as a houseboat with Mrs Barrable, their mother's former teacher. Mrs Barrable is the development of the webfooted grandmother idea. Tom has to hide because he is fleeing from a pursuing motor-cruiser full of Hullabaloos whom he has cast off because they were moored by a favourite coot's nest with eggs about to hatch and it was the only thing he could do to save the chicks. The Hullabaloos had been told by other members of the Coot Club, the Death and Glories, but had refused to move. Soon the *Teasel* becomes a training ship, as Tom's neighbours Port and Starboard Farland and the Death and Glories join forces to help Tom keep clear of the avenging Hullabaloos, and at the same time teach Dick and Dorothea to sail. Tom is chased all over the Broads before the Hullabaloos ram a beacon post on Breydon Water and are salved by the Death and Glories.

The setting of *Coot Club* is remarkably accurate. Unlike the Lake stories where the elements of a real-life landscape are moved around and blended to make a life-like fictional one, Arthur accepted the constraints imposed by reality almost entirely. Tom Dudgeon's house with its golden bream weather vane and waterside lawn is not to be found in Horning reach, although there are several dykes and houses which would make admirable homes for the Farland family. In reality the three Death and Glories would not have been able to have established such an impeccable alibi by weeding in the policeman's garden because in the 1930s Horning was policed by the constable from Ludham.

Mr Farland was clearly a member of Horning Sailing Club and raced a 20ft Yare and Bure One Design. Arthur went strangely adrift with the name, as all the class members are named after butterflies or moths. Perhaps he thought that if he chose a butterfly there would be a clamour of new boatowners to be the first to have the name registered.

Locally it is believed that *Teasel* was one of the sailing cruisers hired out by Percy Hunter's yard at Womak Dyke, Ludham. Perhaps she was just a typical four-berth cabin yacht of the period. Some of the incidents in the story occurred to the Ransomes on that 1934 voyage around the Broads. They met an ice-cream seller at Potter Heigham, towed through Yarmouth, moored close to a Thames barge in Beccles, saw a fisherman with an eel-bab and were towed back through Yarmouth by a tug remarkably like the *Come Along*.

William, Mrs Barrable's pug, was owned by Margaret and Charles Renold who were fishing friends from Cheadle and who had taken a keen interest in the progress of the story.

Hugh Brogan, Arthur's biographer says of *Coot Club*:

"The result was a worthy successor to Winter Holiday. If at times it touches greatness, it is for a reason barely to be glimpsed in Ransome's working notes. In the writing, the war between the bird-protector Tom and the motor-cruising Hullabaloos, with their gramaphone, radio, yachting-caps and beach-pyjamas, became symbolic of the forces contesting the future of the Broads. The more Ransome detailed the society of the Bure, the Thurne and the Waveney the more clearly he showed that more was at stake than the future of a child-outlaw. The book gained greatly in force since Ransome scrupulously accepted the constraints of chronology and geography. The result was a wonderful picture of the Norfolk waters at a crucial moment of transition. The activities of the RSPB had brought back the bitterns, but the day of the wherry was almost over. The lorry, the radio (later, television), the motor-car, agrarian greed, government policy, sewage and artificial fertilisers were going to do more to undermine the social and natural life of the Broads than Ransome began to guess. In life, the Hullabaloos were going to win. That does not make their defeat in fiction less pleasing; it makes Ransome's scrupulous portrayal of the Broads in 1933 all the more valuable and interesting; and it reminds us that the issues he chose to write about were not trivial: especially not to him. As he had loved the old Russia and the traditional Lake District, so he loved the old Norfolk. *Coot Club* and certain passages of *The Big Six* are his vindication of that love."

Pigeon Post which followed in 1935 brought a return to the Lake country and is a land-based affair of gold mining in the fells. But before it was completed he was already thinking of his next book. The Ransomes were established members of the Pin Mill sailing fraternity and he was the proud owner of a 7-ton cutter, the *Nancy Blackett*. She has four berths and measures 28ft overall with a beam of eight feet and was built by David Hillyard, the well-known Littlehampton builder, of sturdy, seamanlike cruisers. Just as *Racundra* and *Swallow* had been translated into print, *Nancy Blackett* was to provide the starting point for an exceptional story.

Some years earlier, when sailing on the Broads with Ernest Altounyan they had drifted out of Yarmouth Harbour. Ernest remembered looking through the thin planking and seeing the sun as through a china cup. The crew of the yacht were to be the Swallows. John was ready to skipper something larger than poor *Swallow* which was sold when the Ransomes left the Lake District. He relished the technical problems. With his customary thoroughness he took *Nancy* across to Holland to test the accuracy of his idea. The voyage turned out to be rather more like the story than he expected for the young man he took as crew turned out to be hopelessly inadequate and he spent 20 hours at the helm before they made their landfall in Holland.

The Swallows and their mother arrive at Pin Mill to await the return of Commander Walker from a tour of duty abroad. They stay at Alma Cottage with Miss Powell. Here Arthur was strictly accurate for Annie Powell lived at Alma

Cottage and let rooms. She did not have the reputation for making omelettes he claimed for her but after publication, readers turned up and expected them. They meet a young man, Jim Brading, sailing *Goblin* to her anchorage off Pin Mill. *Goblin* is, of course *Nancy Blackett*, even to her official number. Arthur describes *Nancy* with great affection and detail. Years later he was to call her "The best little ship I ever sailed in" Jim Brading was probably modelled on Jim Clay whose father wrote for the Manchester Guardian and who was about to go up to Oxford when they first met in 1935.

Jim invites the Swallows to crew for him for a couple of days until they are due to meet their father. They promise not to go outside the harbour. On the second morning after sailing to the harbour mouth, a calm forces them to use the engine which soon runs out of petrol. They anchor on The Shelf and Jim rows ashore for petrol and in his hurry runs head-first into an Eastern Counties bus. He is whisked away to hospital, but the Swallows, still on board the *Goblin*, know nothing of this. A fog closes in and as the tide rises *Goblin* drags her anchor and drifts out to sea on the first of the ebb. The fog lifts, only to be replaced by heavy rain and strong offshore winds. There is nothing for it but to sail on. The following morning they signal for a pilot who takes them into Flushing where their father is in time to make a pierhead jump from his steamer to sail the *Goblin* back to England.

The heart of the book is the unsought voyage and the response of the children, particularly John and Susan, to real danger. Arthur tells the story in a simple, straightforward manner and succeeds in making the children's heroism believable because at all times they respond and behave like children. Many people, including Arthur himself I suspect, consider *We Didn't Mean to go to Sea* (1937) his masterpiece.

The next book was to be completely different. The starting point was that lovely unspoilt area of mud and ever-changing water known as the Walton Backwaters.

Secret Water, which was published in 1939, came from a few days spent there in company with *Lapwing*, the eight-ton cutter belonging to the Busk family. They had met one day at Pin Mill when the children were practising capsizing under the watchful eye of their father. Asking what all the commotion was about, Arthur was told, "Oh, it's only the Busks" This was just the sort of thing to appeal to Arthur who was probably reminded of the time eight years earlier when he had helped teach the Altounyan children to sail. Very soon they were friends.

The Busks lived at The Grange, Chalmondiston, and the children were enthusiastic readers of the Swallows books and had a dinghy *Wizard*, which in the story came to have a change of crew (just as *Mavis/Amazon* had done in *Swallows and Amazons*) and another dinghy *Zip*. *Wizard* was named by John when he exclaimed "Gosh! She's Wizard!" when he first saw her.

When *Lapwing* reached Hamford Water they had with them a blank map like the one in *Secret Water* drawn by Major Busk. They set out to complete the map, as the Swallows do in the story. The parents and Michael, the youngest, sailed *Wizard* and took the food; John and his cousin sailed *Zip*, and Jill and Major Busk's godson sailed "Jo", a borrowed dinghy which hardly sailed at all. After a morning of exploration they met at a pre-arranged spot for lunch, after which the exploration continued until the dinghies returned to base for the evening meal and the filling-in of the map with parts explored that day. After a few days *Nancy Blackett* appeared flying the Jolly Roger with George and Josephine Russell as crew and the party was complete.

Jill, now Mrs Gillian Beever, remembers that the setting was not completely accurate. Blackberry Coast to the north of Secret (Hamford) Water did not exist, nor were there North-east or North-west Passages. The creek leading to Witch's Quay was rather easier to navigate than the Swallows and Nancy found and the creek leading west from Amazon Creek was put in to provide a reason for Titty to delay her crossing of the Red Sea. The young Busks were put into the story as the mud-patterned tribe of savages, the Eels, Daisy, Dum and Dee. Eventually when the book came out it was dedicated to the Busk family.

Some years later after the war when Arthur was at Pin Mill with *Peter Duck* he was a little bothered by some young admirers. He looked across and saw Gillian, just out of uniform, and told the children, "There's Daisy. You go and ask her" As a general rule he was not keen on children and Evgenia became good at protecting him from too much attention. Arthur was partly a child and Gillian remembers that tea was always taken backwards, starting with the most exciting and finishing up with the bread and butter.

Arthur had some characters and the setting but it was to be a complex business before he decided on the plot. The Swallows are marooned with a borrowed dinghy on the largest island and have to make a map of the area. They have the vaguest of blank maps and stern instructions not to go out to sea again. Soon they meet the Mastodon boy who lives in a derelict barge nearby and agrees to be their native guide. Unexpectedly the Amazons arrive, also with a borrowed dinghy. With the news that the Mastodon is expecting the rest of his savage tribe Nancy finds the thought of war much more stimulating than mere mapmaking. By the time they have to leave the map is finished - just, and Nancy has her war, but there is plenty of tension and the introduction of Bridget, joining her elders for the first time, is a welcome relief. Bridget has no idea of the tension around her and is

'Albion' and the old granary, Wroxham, 1965

Tom . . . . ate the sandwiches his mother had given him for his dinner while sitting on the cabin roof of a business wherry, 'Sir Garnett', and talking to Jim Woodall, her skipper.

Coot Club

18

determined to enjoy every minute. In her straightforward, direct way she has the effect of unifying the cast of 13 and it is a great pity she was excluded from the remainder of the series.

During this time up to the start of world war two the Ransomes continued to sail in Broads cruisers, often accompanied by young friends in other boats. Mostly these came from Pin Mill, but in 1938 they were joined by two of the Swallows and Amazons. Taqui and Titty Altounyan sailed a Whippet and proved to be the best of the younger sailors. The Ransomes and most of the other sailed Fairways. Sometimes in the season Arthur would spend a day or two by the river fishing.

Margaret Renold suggested that Arthur should write a detective story. George Owden who had aided the Hullabaloos in *Coot Club* was a suitable villain and after at first resolving that the story would not involve visitor's boats again Arthur wrote his masterly thriller about the casting off of boats. *The Big Six* is set at the end of the summer holidays during which time the Death and Glories have been putting a stove and cabin with bunks into their old boat. Arthur clearly had a particular boat in mind because I found a diagram in one of his notebooks which gives the length as 21ft and the depth as 4ft. This corresponds exactly with the size of one of the boats in a list of regulation lifeboats I found. These additions mean that the Coot Club will be able to keep a better watch over the birds the following spring. George Owden, who is known to steal rare birds eggs to increase his ample pocket money decides to discredit the Coot Club by casting off boats wherever the Death and Glories go. Naturally enough, everyone remembers Tom's affair of the spring and believes the Coots to be guilty. Only with the timely arrival of Dick and Dorothea does the Coot Club start some detective work of their own. The climax is as exciting and satisfying as anything that he wrote. In the course of the story more information about the life in

Broadland and a charming portrait of village life are included. There is a memorable incident when the Death and Glories catch a 30½ pound pike. This was probably inspired by the 21lb pike in the Swan Inn caught by 12 years old Edward Gillard in 1921 which is mentioned in the story. Another incident woven into the story is the visit to the eel man, George Parker, who had his sett near Black Horse Broad. He was not as venerable as Harry Bangate but was Horning eelman for 47 years before retiring just before the war.

There are almost certainly no originals of Joe, Bill and Pete who were introduced in *Coot Club* as interesting minor characters rather as Bill had been in *Peter Duck*. In *The Big Six* they are centre stage and it is clear Arthur felt considerable warmth for the three part-owners of the *Death and Glory*. He had given them full names: Joe Southgate, Bill Jenkins, Pete Woods, although they never appear in the stories. It is an example of how Arthur used to like to know more about his characters than he put into the books.

The Roaring Donkey is not to be found, although exploring the upper Thurne some years ago I discovered the dyke, just as described, but sadly found it ended in the middle of nowhere. Arthur always liked to be living in the area he was writing about and Horning folk remembered the Ransomes staying at the White Gates Hotel (now a private house) in Horning while he was working.

Next came another fantasy. In *Missee Lee* (1941) Captain Flint and the Swallows and Amazons lose the *Wild Cat* by fire in the China Seas. They are captured by Chinese pirates and eventually escape aboard a Chinese junk. The chief delight of the story is the character of Missee Lee herself.

The eleventh book tells of what the D's are up to in the Lake country and the series closed with a tale involving the Swallows, Amazons and D's sailing aboard an old pilot cutter with Captain Flint, *Great Northern?* (1947). Dick spots a great northern diver nesting in Great Britain for the first time somewhere in the Outer Hebrides. Sadly the Coots are not involved.

For almost 40 years there were 12 stories in the series, but there is another. Nobody knew of its existence until Hugh Brogan discovered it in a drawer of the Ransome Room at the Abbot Hall Museum in Kendal, where there is a fascinating collection of manuscripts, books, sketchbooks, flags and artefacts given by Evgenia.

Hugh Brogan has called the story *Coots in the North* and although only the first few chapters exist in what seems to be a first draft, now it is published readers will know Joe, Bill and Pete rather better. In one of his sketchbook, preceding the sketches for his next published book, *The Picts and the Martyrs* (1943) I found a sketch clearly illustrating an incident in *Coots in the North*. Yet the evidence is not conclusive because in the text of *Coots* there are references to Professor Callum learning to sail, an incident forecast in *Picts*. Perhaps the story was abandoned in favour of the Lakes book and continued at a later date but never completed.

It is August and the Death and Glory is moored outside Jonatt's boatshed because the staithe is full. They have nothing to do. The birds can look after themselves and when they help visitors in trouble they get no more than a thank you. Tom and the twins are on holiday and the D's are in the Lakes. They watch a cruiser being loaded on a trailer for a long journey, by Pete's father and other boatbuilders. She is being taken to the lake in the north where the D's are. Following a chance remark by Mrs Barrable, Joe decides that they shall stow away. He almost tricks Bill and Pete into doing so and off they go. When they arrive at the lake they make friends with the cruiser's owner and borrow a dinghy to look for the D's. They meet, but not before the Coots have fallen foul of Nancy Blackett. The fascinating prospect of the tensions and contrasts between the Swallows and Amazons and the Death and Glories remains unfulfilled although there are notes on how the story could develop and end. It is doubtful if we shall ever know for sure why it was abandoned, but there is no doubt of the quality of what there is. It is vintage Ransome.

Arthur Ransome hoisting the Jolly Roger.

(Photo: Arthur Ransome collection)

In the Wake of *Titmouse*, *Teasel* and the *Death and Glory*

The Broads themselves are what remains of water-filled medieval pits made by digging for peat which was used locally as fuel or taken to Norwich. When Ernest Altounyan and Arthur first sailed here the water was sparkling clear, visitors were few and rowing boats with awnings, converted wherries and slender sailing yachts shared the river with the wherries which still had an important part to play in the local economy.

In *Coot Club* the Norfolk and Suffolk Broads were in a period of transition. The increasing number of motor cruisers for hire was bringing a new kind of visitor while the wherries were becoming fewer each year.

Today, due to an increase in phosphate from sewage and nitrate from adjacent farmland, the rivers are cloudy, the Broads are silting up. The algae which has flourished in the nutrient-rich water has shaded the light from aquatic plants, which has in turn brought about a decline in the variety of aquatic animals. Constant stirring-up of the rivers by motor cruisers has made things worse. The Broads Authority "Broads Plan" of 1987 outlines ways in which phosphate levels may be reduced, water quality improved and water plants re-established. Already the situation is improving. In 1981 Cockshoot Broad was cut off from the River Bure by a dam, and 40,000 cubic yards of mud were pumped out. The experiment has been a complete success and the results can be seen by visitors who can park opposite the Ferry Inn and follow the river bank to the dyke and then use the walkway over the marshy ground to the broad. Phosphate levels in the River Ant have fallen and the Broads Authority are considering a similar solution at Barton Broad.

To me the most abrasive change since Ransome's day has been the introduction of the modern motor cruiser in a style quite unlike the traditional Broads craft. These chromium plated plastic bath-tubs not only look out of place but tests have shown that they produce a higher bow wave than traditional wooden hulls and hence cause more bank erosion. The worst culprits though are the day boats which were surely designed for open waters.

After the war the numbers of hire craft rose steadily until 1980. Since then there has been a slow decline more than compensated by the increase in numbers of private craft. In 1985 there were 1780 motor cruisers for hire and 109 auxillary yachts. The following year there were 9319 private craft registered with the Rivers Yare, Bure and Waveney Commissioners.

It is still possible to hire traditional wooden craft from a few yards and the Norfolk County Sailing Base at Hunters Yard, Ludham, has a fleet of lovely cabin yachts which they charter, looking for all the world like *Teasel*. They have a choice of two, three or four berth yachts.

Albion run by the Norfolk Wherry Trust, still sails, but she is of carvel construction instead of the much more usual clinker. At one time there were more than two hundred trading wherries on the Broads. They were general carriers taking cargoes to all the riverside villages, each of which had its staithe. Most wherries were around 50ft in length, carrying up to 40 tons of cargo. The 40ft mast was carefully balanced so that lowering it to go under bridges really was as easy a business as Jim Woodall and Simon made it in *Sir Garnet*. *Albion* was built in 1898 and in the BBC film she did excellent duty as *Sir Garnet*. There never was a wherry named *Sir Garnet*. This came from a military boyhood hero of Arthur's. The other surviving wherries are *Hathor* amd *Solace*. *Hathor* was built in 1905. She has been re-fitted for charter and can carry a party of twelve. She is operated by Peter Bower and Barny Matthews of Wroxham who also have two wherry yachts of similar vintage.

The Norfolk Naturalists Trust is carrying on the good work of the Coot Club's Bird Protection Society. They have their Broadland Conservation Centre at Ranworth and a National Nature Reserve at Hicking Broad. At Hickling there is a water trail, bird hides and a 60ft observation tower. They offer what they call "An Arthur Ransome adventure for all the family"

The bittern has declined in numbers and there is now only a handful of breeding pairs. The Norfolk Naturalists Trust report no booming males have been heard at Hickling for the past three years. The marsh harrier has bred there intermittently and their records show only 23 pairs of bearded tits nested there in 1987. Coots, great crested grebes, swans, herons and mallard are plentiful.

Mr Farland would feel very much at home in Horning today. A fleet of ten or so White Boats, as the Yare and Bure One Designs are known, sail and race regularly at Horning Sailing Club just as they did in the 1930s. The class is still very popular, numbering 111. Of these 101 are still on the racing register, including three of the originals built in 1908. In 1938, four years after the appearance of *Coot Club*, one of the class was named *Grizzled Skipper*, this being the name of the yacht beaten by *Flash* by a bowsprit length at the end of the book. Recent hulls have been built in glass-fibre, but as all the hulls are white, they look fine.

Horning is the centre of the world of the Broadland stories. The Coots sail to Beccles and Potter Heigham but they are, as Dorothea would put it, travellers to foreign parts. Fortunately, although there have been changes, the riverside village of Horning is just as delightful and friendly a place as it was 50 years ago. In the centre of the village, the staithe itself is unchanged. In fact the tap which has replaced the pump on the green is almost the only evidence of progress. How fortunate it was that when the malthouses were pulled down in the 1920s, the parish decided to have a little green beside the staithe!

Just above the staithe The Swan is not quite what it once was, having been extended and altered several times. It remains the focal point for local yachtsmen, who look in for their midday pints just as the boatbuilder fathers of the Coots did. Below the staithe Banham's Boatyard, with its dentist's window overlooking the river has been replaced by some fine riverside houses.

I have seen two or three converted lifeboats looking very much like mastless *Death and Glories* in Horning reach. It would be fascinating to know if Arthur saw one of them when at White Gates while he was at work on *The Big Six*.

Across from the staithe in the village street, Roys Stores, where the Death and Glories had money to burn, is under different ownership these days. The shop is the one which looks as though it was built in the front garden of a thatched cottage near The Swan.

A short way down towards the ferry is White Gates which is now a private house. Any one of the original cottages nearby would do for Mr Tedder's cottage, but Pete's cottage, just around the corner from The Swan has been pulled down. Further down the road a large boatshed stands and could be the one in which Tom and Joe saw the flash of the villain's torch and around a bend in the road the scene can have changed little in the last 50 years. Explorers will look in vain for Dr Dudgeon's house among the dykes and willows on the right-hand side. The location of the *Coot Club* dyke was probably just beyond Chumley and Hawkes Boatyard which has been there since the 1920s. I used to think it was on the site of the yard until I discovered the yard was already established.

In *The Big Six* Arthur mentions the changes between the time of the story (1932) and the time of writing (1940) which occurred to the river bank on what had been the Wilderness. The number of bungalows has further increased and the dyke has been widened and a boatyard has sprung up. Only a narrow strip of Wilderness remains beside the road, but the Wilderness existed and is remembered by local folk who played there in their youth.

It is by the Ferry Inn that the greatest change has taken place. The commercial part of the village has moved from one end to the other and now includes a marina as well as many yards. The present Ferry Inn is not the one in which Bill's aunt worked as this was bombed on April 26th 1941. Four bombs hit the inn and another fell on the ferry pontoon. At the time the bar was crowded and 21 lives were lost and several people seriously injured. The inn was rebuilt but that building was destroyed by fire. The present building occupies a site dating from the eleventh century. The ferry itself was replaced but it has not operated for many years. Below the ferry the ditch where the villains fell after Bill had removed the plank has been widened into the dyke which leads to the marina. It was much quieter when I first moored there in 1956. One morning I looked out of the cabin windows straight into the eyes of a bittern standing on the bank not a yard away. I was so amazed that I forgot all about taking a photograph and just watched it walk towards the river.

There is now no sign of the eelman's old sett by Black Horse Broad, but Horning still has its eelmen who live in houses and not in hulks and whose nets are often seen hanging up to dry on their boats moored by the New Inn. Their modern Fyke nets are not only more efficient, but can be set up where the eel fisher chooses at different states of the tide. Tom Cable, who was fishing for eels at Kendal or Candle Dyke in the 1930s, recalls that he used to fish for a period of five nights when the moon was on the wane. Wet and windy nights when it was particularly dark were considered the best conditions. He fished for mature silver eels. "Stream" eels reach maturity at about ten years, when they turn from yellow to silver underneath. He reckoned that male eels were two to the pound and female eels weighed from a pound and a half to six pounds. Nets were expensive and when it was raised a red light was displayed and during the day notices warned crews of passing vessels not to quant. The net was always raised when the tide was ebbing and was kept in place for five hours. It was lowered after the first of the flood had washed the rubbish back out of the nets.

Almost five miles upstream from Horning are the twin villages of Wroxham and Hoveton. Trains from Norwich still stop at the station and in the village the store where Mrs Barrable bought the D's cheap oilskins has developed out of all recognition. The old bridge remains, but the granary which stood beside it has been replaced by the Riverside Centre. A small boatyard was opened over 100 years ago and it has been suggested that the boat letting industry started here. Even today Wroxham is one of the most important centres and it is still vibrant with activity similar to that which impressed Dick and Dorothea when they arrived.

Downstream from Horning the river meanders past several places where the coot with the white feather could have nested until the narrow dyke leading to Ranworth is reached. Arthur called the broad known today as Malthouse Broad simply Ranworth Broad. Ranworth is a popular port of call and there are usually 20 or so motor cruisers moored stern-on to the staithe. The Maltsters public house stands at the road junction and looks across to the staithe where the old granary has been replaced by a supermarket and information centre. Nearby there is a children's play area and a nature trail leading to the nature reserve of Ranworth Broad and its Conservation Centre. Up the hill a little way is the Post Office which Dick and Dorothea visited to send picture postcards home. It is all very pleasant, but Ranworth today is not the quiet backwater where Tom lay low or the Death and Glories tried to emigrate from their troubles.

Explorers should not miss the River Ant just because it hardly features in the books. It is very much Ransome country with its reed fringed banks and meadowland. A five miles per hour speed limit operates throughout its length and perhaps this helps to keep it noticeably quiter than the River Bure. At How Hill there is an Environmental and Field Study Centre devoted to the traditional Broadland way of life and the wildlife of the area. In this part of the Broads the swallowtail butterfly can be seen and at night the occasional booming of the bittern is heard.

The River Thurne will seem familiar to Ransome readers. Potter Heigham bridge provides its age-old challenge to helmsmen and where the railway bridge used to cross, a new road bridge takes through traffic away from the old bridge. Readers can follow the rond and try to decide just where the world's whopper was caught. Above the bridge is a lovely, wild part of the Broads. Hickling Broad and Horsey Mere await the sailor who can try quanting where Dick fell in and if there is room moor in the dyke by the windmill as *Teasel* did.

Voyagers to the south pass through one bridge fewer in Yarmouth these days. Anyone in trouble can still contact the Yacht Station who contact reliable watermen like the owner of the *Come Along*. Across the entrance to Breydon Water the railway bridge has been replaced by a modern road bridge. Beyond the bridge the great expanse of Breydon Water and its two lines of posts have not changed. At the far end the Berney Arms still stands in splendid isolation but in the New Cut there is no need for anyone to hold out the butterfly net to collect tolls for passing under the lifting road bridge. Hot baths are still available at the Yacht Station at Oulton Broad which is a very popular stretch of water and looks very unlike the photographs the Ransomes took on their visit.

Beccles is still a very pleasant town. The malthouses have largely gone from beside the staithe, but the road leading up into the town was as clear as in Arthur's drawing when I walked up it one Sunday morning. On the right-hand side the narrow passages called scores lead down to the river just as in *Coot Club*. The road leads up to the church where the old wall still looks out over the river. At Beccles I came across a mystery I could not solve. *Teasel* moored at the public staithe which is easy to find. But the *Welcome of Rochester* was moored on the other side of the river. Here William rummaged in the straw of the mill staithe, later called the quay, by Beccles Mill. I asked several people in Beccles where the mill used to be and they all said that there never was any mill on that side of the river and also that when Thames barges called at Beccles, which they did quite often, they moored at the public staithe like *Teasel*. Neither Beccles Library nor the Local History Society had any evidence of any mill on that bank. I cannot think of any reason why the mill should have been moved to satisfy the demands of the story. Still, as Peggy once said, "It only spoils things to be too beastly clever."

In the Wake of *Goblin*, *Wizard* and *Firefly*

Pin Mill has changed very little since Nancy Blackett and Lapwing lay at their moorings in the river. The car park is small and unobtrusive and the picnic area pleasantly set out. The waterfront itself looks very like the illustrations Arthur drew so carefully. The sixteenth-century Butt and Oyster provides splendid "Breakfasts" for today's Jim Bradings and the interior appears much as it did in the days when it was the haunt of working sailormen. Sitting in the old bow window of the bar while the high tide laps the wall a few feet below is an experience Ransome admirers will long remember.

Nearby, three adjoining cottages Alma Cottage, Riverside Cottage and Seagulls were formerly the Alma Inn. This was sold by Cobbolds, the Ipswich brewers, in 1910. It was bought by Annie Powell in 1918 and she lived there until her death in the 1950s. It is almost certain that in the days when Arthur was writing the present properties were still one and Annie Powell was living with her unmarried brother Jack. He made the sails for the Thames barges in the sail loft next door, in what is now the yacht chandlers. After his marriage he and his wife occupied the part which is now Seagulls. Alma is a holiday cottage, but at Riverside Cottage climbing roses still cling to the wall where the windows look out on a scene where land, in comparison to water, still seems hardly to matter at all. Hetty Watts, who has the good fortune to look out through those windows, told me she often hears cries of "There's Alma Cottage!" in the lane outside, from readers making their first visit.

The hard in front of the Butt goes out a long way at low water but dinghies use the stream which runs beside it just as *Wizard* does in *Secret Water*. The stream, or Grindle as it is called, silts up and has to be cleared out by hand each year.

Harry King's boatyard no longer builds wooden boats, but they seem to have plenty of repair work and fitting out to do and occasionally they complete a fibre-glass hull. The yard is still in the family, being run by Harry's grandson Geoff. Harry King's son Sam, now retired, told me how he remembers *Selina King* and *Peter Duck* being built. Arthur spent much time at the yard during the building of *Selina King* and planned to write a book about her building. Evgenia chose the name *Selina* and when Harry King heard, he told Arthur that he had an aunt of that name. "Then we shall call her *Selina King*," replied Arthur. Sam built Arthur a tiny dinghy, the *Queen Mary*, as a tender to *Nancy*. In those days dinghies were built by eye without plans, using a couple of moulds which were removed after the timbers were fastened. With the outbreak of war Harry King set aside some timber for Arthur and Major Busk to build yachts when it was all over. This explains how *Peter Duck* was built so soon after hostilities had ceased, when timber was in very short supply.

Peter Duck is in very good shape and is now based at Woodbridge. *Nancy Blackett* has been at Scarborough for a number of years and has been well looked after. She has recently suffered from some unfortunate damage below the waterline and from the effects of a car which feel on her from the quay where she was moored. By one of those strange coincidences, she has just been bought by Michael Rines who lives not much more than an arrow's flight from the Ransome's old home at Broke Farm. She is still sound, but in need of considerable repair and it would be fitting if she were to be repaired by King's yard. It should not be too long before she will be sailing off Pin Mill again and Michael Rines has some exciting plans for her which include an appearance at the International Boat Show, a re-enactment of the famous voyage to Holland with a child crew and charter to Ransome enthusiasts so they could sail to *Secret Water*. Ideas which I think would have Arthur chuckling with approval.

Arthur and Evgenia spent five happy years at Pin Mill. In the Lakes he always lived in isolation in remote cottages, but here he had a number of local friends including several families of children who helped him with the winter work on *Nancy*. As well as the Busks there were the Russells - George and Josephine - who often sailed as his crew.

The Orwell with its wooded banks is a beautiful river. Many more people are able to use it these days since the opening of the marinas at Levington, Woolverstone and Shotley. A few small tugs fuss up the river to Ipswich but the large ships have bow and stern thrusters and can manoeuvre themselves. Helmsmen are no longer distracted by the sight of porpoises bobbing up in the river, perhaps due to pollution and increased traffic.

Down river the Felixstowe bank has altered beyond recognition. The old part has been swallowed up by the huge container port. More than two miles of container termini are served by container transit areas upwards of half a mile in depth. In the midst of this the old Felixstowe Dock is almost hidden. It used to be at the end of a public road which led to the mills, bus terminus, sheds, the Pier Hotel and a few houses. Now the approach to the ferry is down a heavily caged-in footpath through the dock complex. Beside the old dock stand some of the mills seen from the *Goblin* and the Pier Hotel, which now bears the name Little Ships Hotel, but contains offices. The rank commercialism of the port and the sheer functional lines of the ships have stripped the place of all romance. Arthur would hate it. Downstream is the old Landguard fort which has stood guarding the harbour mouth since the seventeenth century.

Off Landguard Point is the Beach End buoy. It no longer has the wave-actuated bell which puzzled the crew of the *Goblin*. This was shifted to its neighbour the North-west Beach buoy when massive dredging operations eased the right-angle bend into the harbour, around which the huge container vessels could not go. It has changed colour since the inernationally agreed buoyage system came into operation in 1977, when it was painted green. The sound of the Cork lightship's beu....eueueueueu no longer warns mariners in the harbour of mist along the coast, as the lightship was removed some years ago and the area is now marked by lighted buoys.

Across the water Harwich has fared better. The town is a happy blend of old and new and its skyline is little changed and still dominated by the spire of St Nicholas Church. On the Quay, opposite Ha'penny Pier, the old Town Hall, into which Jim Brading hurried to find the Harbour Master for news of his missing ship, is being re-developed. The Harbour Master now has his own building on the river's edge which houses the Port Control Station and is topped by aerials and radar scanners. It is all so much more organised these days.

The ferryboat *Brightlingsea* is probably the only remaining link with Ransome's day, for she has been around since 1925. Although converted from steam to diesel many years ago she is recognisable as the small, dumpy boat the Swallows watched while waiting for Jim to return. She is run by the Orwell and Harwich Navigation Company Limited and runs between Harwich and Felixstowe Dock, as well as making harbour cruises. Land-based Ransome enthusiasts will find a ferry cruise an excellent way to explore.

Up the river Stour ferries operate between Parkeston Quay and Esbjerg and the Hook, but they look more like "engines in tin boxes"tthan anything the Swallows had ever seen when John dismissed steam on the first page of *Swallows and Amazons.*

Shotley still has its wooden piers, but there is no longer any employment for Lieutenant-Commanders, as HMS Ganges closed some years ago. The new marina has brought life back to that side of the river and some new housing and a sports complex has replaced the naval establishment. Off the pier a couple of sad red lightships lie on the old Trinity House steamer moorings and further up the river a group of lightships, now redundant, wait for somebody to decide what to do with them.

For all the changes the container port has brought about, Orwell Haven is still a glorious sheltered stretch of water, which becomes full of little ships on summer weekends when yachts come down from Pin Mill and the marinas.

A little careful navigation will bring seaborne explorers to the entrance of Secret Water. Away to port, Amazon Creek is quite a highway leading to moorings down near Walton and the Tichmarsh Marina around Cape Horn. The rest of the secret archipelago is delightfully quiet and peaceful. Quiet that is except for the constant chatter of the gulls.

In *Secret Water* Arthur, who was so careful with technical details and who delighted in solving technical problems, avoided all reference to spring or neap tides. Channels which are navigable by dinghies on spring tides are impassable at other times. In this part of the east coast spring tides occur when high water is about 2 pm yet *Wizard* and *Firefly* made their passages when high water was at nine o'clock in the morning. The scene Arthur describes with the water right up to the saltings ocurs with spring tides. Martin Lewis has spent many holidays exploring and he sent me his fascinating illustrated logs. He has navigated the North-west Passage and he feels it may be possible to do the North-east Passage on a high spring tide although he has not yet succeeded. Whether there was a Blackberry Coast 50 years ago I have not been able to establish. The present charts look as if there may have been an island there, which has suffered from erosion by high tides in the same way as Mastodon Island.

One or two yachts anchor off Flint Island just as *Lapwing* did, but *Goblin's* old anchorage off Swallow Island is now oyster beds. In the channel betwwen Bridget Island and Mastodon Island and the mainland there are several delightful moorings,

Explorers on land can leave their car in a park near the Naze tower and walk along the cliffs and round a nature reserve until Amazon Creek is reached. Flint Island's sandy shore is clearly visible to the north and in the other direction the seawall leads up the creek towards Walton. Walton itself is a pleasant small seaside town which looks as though it has not changed too much through the years. The Eels' instructions for finding the boatbuilders can be followed without trouble and near to the boatbuilders is the head of Amazon Creek.

A little over a mile down the road to Kirby Le Soken, a lane by a farm leads to the Red Sea. At the lane's end it rises over the sea wall to reveal an inland sea, or a path leading across an expanse of mud. At low water the road leads temptingly towards Swallow Island. It is just as Arthur described it: a firm gravel base covered by puddles and a layer of soft mud.

The four posts in the middle have gone, although several withies mark the way. Recently I followed a smartly dressed rider as her horse splashed across to the island and I spotted some bait diggings like those which puzzled Titty and Bridget. The causeway seems to be well-used, for one Ransome enthusiast told me that when he went across to explore Swallow Island he had to wait for a furniture van to cross!

A footpath along the sea wall leads from the Wade towards Witch's Quay. I have visited Witch's Quay several times and each time I have been aware of a sense of timelessness. It is as if the world has forgotten the old barge quay and its granary. Civilisation seems miles away, although it is lurking just out of sight down the lane. The witch's cottage is in good repair and at the end of the lane stands a house with a glorious view across the saltings to Swallow Island. I hope the old granary, which for some years has been a house, will be repaired and lived in again.

The marks which were so confusing to the map makers must have been spotted by Arthur somewhere or other, but they are no good for marking creeks which dry out at half tide and below. If the line from the buoy to the mooring is long enough to let them float at high water, as the tide goes out they float further and further from the channel they are supposed to mark. Withies are the only answer.

Mastodon Island is now a nature reserve and the warden has replaced the Mastodon as the island's only inhabitant. Like Swallow Island, it is linked to the mainland by a causeway. The area south west of Mastodon Island is much more interesting than the Secret Archipelago Expedition's map suggests. Martin Lewis carried on where they left off and has mapped it most carefully.

Two or three Thames barges have rotted away in Secret Water. Gillian Beevor could not remember *Speedy* from her

map-making trip, but Jim Clay told Christina Hardyment that he did remember a barge which had one end turned into a cabin.

A couple of years ago Brigit Sanders had the opportunity to make her first visit to Secret Water. I was very interested to read her account of the trip.

"Friends who keep a boat at Bradwell recently organized a 'return' visit to Secret Water for me.

"Compare the chart of Walton Backwaters with the map of Secret Water in the book and you will see how similar they are. Our skipper Paul pointed to Mastodon Island. A borrowed mooring was waiting there...just where George the seal had appeared. But our first objective was Pin Mill. Paul and Margaret had it all arranged. Sea sailing was going to be a new experience for me and I was excited at the prospect.

"From Bradwell we made for Woolverston Marina, sailing through the Wallet and up the river Orwell in a stiff breeze. Uncle Arthur had moved to Levington from the Lakes and had written *Secret Water* about 50 years ago. What had changed for the sailor since then I wondered?

"Our craft was a 30 foot motor sailing boat with a fibreglass hull and all manner of electronic aids. The boat itself was the first evidence of change since Ransome sailed *Nancy Blackett* in these waters. Soon we met a string of Thames barges. In the thirties they were cargo boats and among the few craft Ransome would encounter. The barges we met were pleasure boats returning from an annual race. They were still as beautiful as ever. At Woolverston we tied up alongside one. Lying there, as it were in repose, with brown sails furled, she reminded me of a praying mantis.

"Once we turned up the Orwell we were very conscious of the traffic. Huge Channel ferries and container ships

'Pommern'

Coming out beyond the 'Cork' was one of the last of the old sailing ships, a four-masted barque, being towed out clear of the shoals before setting sail for the Baltic.

(Photo: Arthur Ransome, courtesy Martin Lewis)

We Didn't Mean to go to Sea

towered over us. Fishing trawlers swept us aside and a mass of moored yachts provided us with an obstacle course. The river was no longer the place for a lone sailor like Uncle Arthur.

"Woolverstone Marina was our first stop. I realized what big business yachting is these days and couldn't help thinking that Uncle Arthur's books had some small part to play in this booming activity. All the sports we indulged in as children were done in total isolation, but we were keen none the less. In the Marina I found myself in a 'Yachting World' Had some magic and excitement gone?

"After supper we walked to Pin Mill through ripening corn full of poppies to visit Alma Cottage. The present occupants just had to be Ransome fans. We looked out from their living room on a view that can't have changed much in these 50 years. The Butt and Oyster on the right. King's yard on the left. Glancing at the book shelf beside me I noticed a complete set of Ransome's books.

"The entrance to Secret Water could still easily be missed by a skipper unfamiliar with this coast line. Our skipper was well briefed, so we slipped through the entrance to these inland waters and found ourselves in a different world. The uncomplicated landscape of water, reeds, distant clumps of trees and islands reminded me instantly of the Antioch marshes where we alone sailed, in our amber dinghy *Peter Duck*. Here there was the added interest of tidal waters where masts of boats appeared and disappeared beyond the banks of reeds.

"Our hosts were excellent organisers. After picking up our mooring off Mastodon Island, we stood on deck to admire our surroundings. Suddenly Margaret gripped my arm and pointed. Something had broken the surface of the water. George it could not be, but his distant cousin had come to say hallo. The skipper said nothing; but I thought I saw a satisfied look on his face.

"I'm glad to say that when the inevitable happened and the weather broke, the ship's baby-cum-granny did not hang miserably over the gunwale but kept her sea legs. Due to the weather we had an extra night at Woolverston and so were able to watch the racing of the Royal Harwich. Today's ships babies were running around in shoals preparing for their race. "I'm sailing an OPTIMIST" said one little girl. Uncle Arthur would not have enjoyed sharing these waters with the container ships but would, I'm sure, have joined in the enthusiasm of these young skippers."

It seems to me that Brigit is right. East Anglia has changed in many respects during the last 50 years, but what matters is that more people are looking after the wildlife, fishing, sailing and exploring the places her Uncle Arthur loved and doing those things of which he thoroughly approved.

The Northern Broads

Horning Staithe 1962

The staithe? Everyone knows the staithe, where boats tie up when calling at Horning.

Everyone knows the inn at the bend of the river above it, . . .

and the boatbuilders sheds below it, . . .
(Photo: courtesy George Southgate)

. . . and the bit of green grass beside it, and the pump by the old brick wall, and the road with the shops on the further side of it.

The Big Six

'Jonnatt's' the boatbuilders

Joe, Bill and Pete were sitting on the cabin top of the 'Death and Glory'. They had tied up to the posts outside Jonnatt's, the boatbuilders, because there was no room along Horning Staithe. Hired sailing boats and motor cruisers were tied up all along the staithe, from the wall of the inn garden down to Jonnatt's.

Coots in the North

Horning Reach, 1956

The 'Death and Glory' was on her way, water rippling under her bows, the tow-rope taut, chug-chug sounding from the 'Cachalot's' engine, and the well-known banks of the home reach slipping by on either side.

"Nobody's going to come waking us tonight," said Bill.

It was as if in leaving Horning they were leaving their troubles behind.

The Big Six

Above the Ferry, 1957

There have been changes in the last few years along the banks above the Ferry, and one or two neat bungalows have been built on what was once the Wilderness, a marshy bit of land with an old wind-pump on it, a lot of osier bushes and a narrow dyke running through it from the river to the road.

The Big Six

The Ferry

And then just as he shot past the Ferry, he saw George Owden leaning on the white-painted rail of the ferry-raft and looking down at him.

Coot Club

Below the Ferry, 1956

Below the Ferry and about thirty yards below the narrow, deep ditch that keeps cattle from straying off the meadows, the six detectives and William (who was a little out of breath and lay panting, showing his pink tongue) waited for the 'Cachalot'.

The Big Six

Pete's cottage, 1971

"Think they'll drag the river?" said Joe. Bill did not answer and they ran grimly on, round the corner by the inn, and so to the row of cottages, one of which was Pete's home.

The Big Six

Horning Lower Street, 1988

They had come as far as the first of the big boatsheds that lay between the road and the river.

The Big Six

Eelmen's boats of the 1980s by the New Inn, Horning, with a Fyke net drying in the sun.

(Photo: courtesy George Southgate)

(right) **By the Wilderness, 1972**

Dr Dudgeon listened carefully. Presently he stepped over the fence. The others scrambled over and took him through the bushes to the 'Death and Glory'.

The Big Six

Wroxham Bridge, 1920s

(left) **I found this ex-lifeboat in a dyke at Horning in the 1970s. She was about the same size as the 'Death and Glory', with a similar cabin.**

There were boats everywhere, and boats of all kinds, from the big black wherry with her gaily painted mast, loading at the old granary by Wroxham bridge, and meant for nothing but hard work, to the punts of the boatmen going to and fro, and the motor-cruisers filling up with petrol, and the hundreds of big and little sailing yachts tied up to the quays, or moored in rows, two and three deep, in the dykes and artificial harbours beside the main river.

Coot Club

River Bure, 1957

On they went, past the vicarage with the waterhens and the black sheep on the lawns by the waterside.

The Big Six

Ranworth Broad

Half way along the dyke they came on a couple of men loading reeds into a reed-boat and they waited while Tom rowed 'Titmouse' into a good position for Dick to take a photograph.

The Big Six

'The Malsters', Ranworth, 1972

"Well, I think no good my going off without seeing young Rob, so I wait a bit and make a round and come back and I don't see nobody until I come down by the Malster's, and there were that young Rob on the staithe, and you wouldn't believe it but that young Rob run away."

The Big Six

'Hathor', 1988

'Sir Garnet' was the fastest trading wherry on the river.

The Big Six

(Photo: courtesy George Southgate)

Eel Fisher's Hut

(Photo: courtesy George Southgate)

Potter Heigham Bridge

They came to the boatyards of Potter Heigham, and the staithe and the lovely old bridge built four hundred years ago and maybe more.

Coot Club

(Photo: Arthur Ransome)

Under the Arch, 1956

But there was no chance to change helmsmen. The 'Cachalot' was already nosing in under the arch. The 'Death and Glory' followed her.

The Big Six

Ice Cream Seller, Potter Heigham

The others took William for a walk, and, on the way back met a "Stop me and buy one" ice-cream boy on his bicycle. They stopped him and bought seven, of which one was wasted because it was strawberry and William decided that he did not care for any but vanilla.

Coot Club

(Photo: Arthur Ransome)

River Thurne

"I can steer now," said Dick, as they came out on the other side and he saw the railway bridge ahead of them, crossing the river with a single span.

Coot Club

(Photo: probably Evgenia Ransome)

River Thurne, 1988

The morning mist was heavy on the river and on the sodden field that lay on either side of it. The fields were below the level of the river and the Death and Glories, marching along the rond that kep the river from overflowing, looked down on feeding cattle and horses whose thick coats were pale with moisture.

The Big Six

Breydon Rail Bridge

Through Breydon Bridge the 'Come Along' towed them, and round the dolphins and into the mouth of the North River, where the tide was running up.

Coot Club

(Photo: Arthur Ransome)

The mouth of the River Bure with the road bridge across Breydon Water, 1988.

Lowestoft North Quay, 1988

*At that moment Peter Duck tapped his
pipe out on his bollard, got up, walked
to the edge of the quay and
said, "Cap'n."*

Peter Duck

River Waveney at Beccles, 1988

*Under the bridges they could see the
curving river, houses almost standing
in the water, rowing boats tied up to
the walls, and a flock of white ducks
swimming from one back door to the
next.*

*"Brother Richard was quite right,"
said the Admiral. "This is much the
best way to see it again."*

Coot Club

Beccles

Romance came to life again as, after a last look at the 'Teasel' and the distant barge, they left the staithe and walked up the long street into the town.

Coot Club

Oulton Broad, 1988

"Hot Baths!" exclaimed Mrs Barrable, and there, on the quay, by the harbour-master's office, Dorothea saw the notice and pointed it out. "Hot baths, 1s."

Coot Club

Pin Mill

Pin Mill, 1988

Last night they had slept for the first time at Alma Cottage, and this morning had waked for the first time to look out through Miss Powell's climbing roses at this happy place . . .

Pin Mill, 1972

. . . where almost everybody wore seaboots, and land, in comparison with water, seemed hardly to matter at all.

We Didn't Mean to go to Sea

52

Alma Cottage, 1988

They were just following daddy up the steps to Alma Cottage when Titty saw a woman coming down tht lane and waving to them. She stopped.

"Isn't this for your mother?" said the woman, holding out a letter. Postman left it at mine by mistake."

Secret Water

'Lapwing' at Pin Mill

"Pudding faces," said Roger. "They're probably going somewhere and we're not."

Secret Water

(Photo: Arthur Ransome)

53

(left) **River Orwell, 1988**

The others had no heart for boats, and went for a walk along the woods above the river. But even there they could not forget what had happened. Yachts were coming up the river. Yachts were going down. Each one of them was going somewhere or coming back.

Secret Water

'Nancy Blackett' (Photo: Arthur Ransome)

Evgenia Ransome at the tiller of 'Nancy Blackett'.

(Photo: Arthur Ransome)

The North Shelf Buoy, 1988

The pierheads, dim and shadowy, were swallowed up in the fog. For a few minutes they could still see the North Shelf Buoy. Then that too disappeared.

We Didn't Mean to go to Sea

(Photo: Victor Steynor)

Harwich and the North Shelf Buoy, 1988

He dodged round a railway truck and a heap of coal, and looked across the harbour, and looked, and looked again.

She had gone.

We Didn't Mean to go to Sea

Felixstowe Mills, 1988

Far away over blue rippled water they could see tall mills by Felixstowe Dock.

We Didn't Mean to go to Sea

(Photo: Victor Steynor)

Felixstowe Dock

They watched the little black dinghy disappear between the pierheads into Felixstowe Dock.

We Didn't Mean to go to Sea

(top left) **The 'Brightlingsea', 1988**

"Here's the ferryboat again. Gosh, won't it be fun when we all go to meet Daddy?"

We Didn't Mean to go to Sea

(left) **Redundant lightship off Shotley and yachts on the Orwell, 1988**

(above) **Brigit Altounyan, in a portrait by her mother.**

The Walton Backwaters

Secret Water, 1988

*"Why is your totem an eel?" said Titty.
"Mud everywhere," said the Mastodon. "Eels like it and so do
we."*

Secret Water

Red Sea at High Water, 1988

*The shores were widening on either side, and they were coming
out in a broad lake of shimmering water which covered the sea
of mud that they had seen in the morning.*

Secret Water

Swallow Island from the Middle of the Red Sea, 1988

The road was much better than they had expected. There were deep puddles in it, left by the tide. There was a layer of soft mud over it, but never deep enough to cover their ankles. Under the mud there was good hard gravel, and it was easy walking, though they found it best not to walk too near together, because nobody could help splashing the mud about. There was nothing but mud on each side of the road and Roger, just trying whether it was hard or soft, very nearly lost a boot in it.

Secret Water

Witch's Quay Creek, 1987

From the top of the quay they looked back and, far away over the water, could see the roof of the native kraal on Swallow Island. "Gosh!" said Nancy, "It looks simple enough from up here."

Secret Water

Witch's Cottage, 1988

Away to the left was a broken down wooden fence, with a wicket gate in it, and beyond it a thatched cottage, a very small cottage of tarred black wood standing in a small potato patch.

Secret Water

Bridget Island and Goblin Creek, 1988

They were passing the little Bridget Island that at low water was part of their own.

Secret Water

Fifty years on another generation of young explorers about to land on Flint Island where the Swallows and Amazons landed on their way to rescue Bridget. Moored in 'Lapwing's' Place is a very splendid dhow - Richard Woodman's 97 year old cutter 'Kestrel' which had moored near 'Nancy Blackett' at Pin Mill in the 1930s.

(Photo: Richard Woodman)

(left) **The Head of Amazon Creek, 1973**

"You can get right up to the town at high water in a dinghy. But if you do, don't wait there too long, or there won't be water to take you back," (said Daddy).

Secret Water

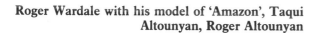

Roger Wardale with his model of 'Amazon', Taqui Altounyan, Roger Altounyan

(Photo: Brigit Sanders)

Bibliography

The two main sources of Ransome material are to be found in the Brotherton Collection at the University of Leeds and the Ransome Collection at the Abbot Hall Museum, Kendal.

Altounyan, Taqui *In Aleppo Once* (John Murray, 1969)

Beesley, Julia *What to do on the Norfolk Broads* (Jarrold, 1988)

Broads Authority *Broads Plan* (1987)

Broads Authority *Ranworth Staithe Case Study* (1983)

Brogan, Hugh *The Life of Arthur Ransome* (Jonathan Cape, 1984)

Coote, Jack *East Coast Rivers from the Air* (Yachting Monthly)

Hardyment, Christina *Arthur Ransome and Captain Flint's Trunk* (Jonathan Cape, 1984)

Hay, David and Joan *East Anglia from the Sea* (Stanford, 1972)

Ransome, Arthur *Peter Duck* (Jonathan Cape, 1932)

Ransome, Arthur *Coot Club* (Jonathan Cape, 1934)

Ransome, Arthur *We Didn't Mean to go to Sea* (Jonathan Cape, 1937)

Ransome, Arthur *Secret Water* (Jonathan Cape, 1939)

Ransome, Arthur *The Big Six* (Jonathan Cape, 1940)

Ransome, Arthur *Autobiography* (Jonathan Cape, 1976) (Edited and with prologue and epilogue by Sir Rupert Hart-Davis)

Ransome, Arthur (Ed. Hugh Brogan) *Coots in the North and Other Stories* (Jonathan Cape, 1988)

Stephens, George *100 Pictures of the Norfolk Broads* (Jarrold, 1927)